Heartbeat Serenade

BY: Tanae Morris

Copyright © 2024 by Tanae Morris.

All rights reserved. No part of this book may be used or reproduced in any form whatsoever without written permission except in the case of brief quotations in critical articles or reviews.

Printed in the United States of America/ Canada
Publish by COJ BOOKZ

ISBN: 978-1-998120-35-2

DEDICATION

To: A Lover from another mother You have my undying love. You have me forever.

You are my life's brightness, my heart's rhythm, and my soul's melody.

"Said we were just friends,

Now got me remin',

Remin' and missing you,

Wishing you were here with me right now,

Baby Boo boo boo,

Got me waiting on you,

You know we gon' slide through through through,

I call this kinda thing love love love,

We said we weren't gonna hook up up up,

But I guess we changed our minds,

Now we're stuck together like glue.

Remin' and missin',

Remin' and missin' you,

Said we were just friends,

Now you got me remin' and,

Remin' and missin' you you you.

Let me take you out to my spot,

Get some food, let's relax,

Chill out, where we gonna be at,

That's my way to show my love,

You know we ain't break up,

You were callin' old dude papi, now you callin' me daddy, who jealous of me now,

I'm gonna take you out where your fav spot be at.

Said we were just friends,

Now you got me remin' and,

Remin' and missin' you,

Thinkin' about you 24/7,

Got you on my mind."

We acknowledged our friendship,

Now I find myself reminiscing,

Reflecting and missing you,

Standing by for your presence in this moment,

My love, Patiently awaiting your arrival,

Our plans to come together,

This feeling, I label as love,

Initially, we vowed not to move up,

Yet here we are, inseparable like glue.

Reflecting and missing,

Recalling and aching for you,

What started as a slow friendship,

Now fills me with memories and desire,

Reminiscing and missing you.

Allow me to escort you to a special spot,

Share a meal and unwind,

Relax in the place we've chosen,

My gesture to express affection,

Our bond remains unbroken,

Once you addressed another with endearment,

Now you turn to me with admiration,

I'll take you to your preferred destination.

Acknowledging our friendship,

I find myself reminiscing,

Reflecting and missing you,

Constantly in my thoughts,

You occupy my mind all the time.

If mi tell you x3

Mi ah gon mek you mi lifeline

Mi ah gon mek you mi valentine

So come whine pon mi pipeline

I'm tryna love pon you all night

If mi tell come over right now

what you gonna say

if mi tell yuh tek a place

tek a moment fi breathe now

what you gonna say if mi ask you to be mine

Mi ah gon mek you mi life line

Mi ah gon mek you mi valentine

So come whine pon mi pipeline

I'm tryna love pon you all night

Lemme ask you a question

Lemme ask you right now

Would you tell me It's a yes or a no

If you would be my lady

Mi ah gon mek you mi life line

Mi ah gon mek you mi valentine

So come whine pon mi pipeline

I'm tryna love pon you all night

You kno mi a gon treat you better than he

You kno mi gon tek care of you if we

You kno i got your back baby

I know you want to be my lady

Mi ah gon mek you mi life line

Mi ah gon mek you mi valentine

So come whine pon mi pipeline

I'm tryna love pon you all night

You know Mt pon di ting

you know that you can't run from me

you kno mi ah gon mek

you mine one way or di next

In the rhythm of the night,

My heart has a wonderful delight,

Telling you repeatedly,

You're my lifeline, my peace.

Wanting to dance,

with someone special,

In the moon's soft shine,

Asking you to be mine,

In this lovely moment.

With promises deep and true,

I'll cherish and care for you,

No shadows, no lies,

Just love in my eyes.

So answer me now, with grace,

In this dance, our embrace,

For you are my Valentine,

In this love, pure and fine.

You. You. Baby, me, and you. You.

I'm tryna be with you Baby you

But I feel like you're playing with me.

Yeah. Me, baby. Baby, just watch me and see.

It's for me. It's for you. I'm doing this for us.

Us. Ian tryna be with no hoe baby girl

you already know I'm doing this for us

Baby, just watch me and see.

I'm not putting us in. Whatever nonsense this is.

Baby, it's constant bullshit. Just watch and you'll see.

Babygirl I'm trying to be with you be for us

Baby, just watch it and see. It's for me. It's for you.

I know you want this bad with me, baby me.

But will you watch me and see it's for me it's us

Baby girl, you already know.

We not both hoes. This is the real us.

Baby, please don't hurt me. Baby, just listen to me.

Me. Yeah me I'm tryna be with you yeah you baby you

" Love shouldn't be played with, it should be a bond that's real. It's a live and learn experience sometimes it works sometimes it doesn't you just have to find your person and teach them how to love you" ~ Taelations

Let me show you what I'm really about
Let me take you back to your house
Ian tryna diss you like dat but
You know them boys was some caps
I already been there before messed
With some lames that's really my bad
Fuck alla dat I really got you
Stuck in my head I'm just tryna
Show you around take all
The time you need cuz
Baby It's only 1 MT
I'm not even Tryna waste
no time let me
Pour my heart my soul out
But hold on let me switch
The flow for some soul now
I'm not trying to waste no time
But you know that your always
On my mind I can't even figure
This out what type of feeling
That I'm feeling it's like
You got some spell over me
But you never know how its
Going to end I wasn't even
Searching for no one until I
Seen you and you caught
My eyes so let's break the
Silence cuz you know I'm
Real silent I gotta teach you
How to love me this doesn't
Come very easy take your
Time with me let's enjoy
The ride In this spell you've cast,
you're always on my mind,
No time wasted,it's just you and me,

Exploring these feelings, what could it be?
You caught my eyes, now let's see,
Where this journey leads, just you and me
I'm not holding back, I gotta let you know,
In this spell you've cast on me,
Now I gotta let my feelings show,
You're always on my mind, and I can't let go,
No time wasting, it's just us and we
Gotta let it grow x4 let me take it back to the top
And show you what I really got
Let's take it slow and enjoy the show

Starting fresh, being real, Loving every moment, our love won't conceal.
You've got me on a hook, it's so clear, Thinking of you all year.
It's just us, no wasting time, Exploring our love, making it prime.
Let's keep this love cycle a dime, Our hearts laced, in this love fight.
You're on my mind everyday, Just the two of us, finding our way.

" Building in relationships takes time but once you are patient it goes by. Just be true to yourself then it'll come easy with others. When your true to yourself you'll be more aware of how you feel and you'd connect on a deeper level with people" ~ Taelations

Take time to show yourself and others love by saying:

Confidence and Clarity: "I confidently show you my true self, expressing my feelings with clarity and honesty."

Embracing Connection: "I embrace the connection we share, enjoying each moment as we explore our feelings together."

Openness and Vulnerability: "I open my heart and soul, allowing myself to be vulnerable in this journey of love and discovery."

Appreciation of Time: "I appreciate every moment spent with you, taking the time to nurture our bond and cherish our experiences."

Growth and Exploration: "Our journey together is a beautiful exploration of emotions and growth, where we learn and evolve with each other."

Gratitude for Love: "I am grateful for the love we share, knowing that it enriches my life in profound ways."

Embracing the Unknown: "I embrace the uncertainty of our future, confident that our love and connection will guide us forward."

Living in the Present: "I live fully in the present moment with you, savoring each instance of joy, laughter, and affection."

Commitment to Understanding: "I commit to understanding and learning about you, striving to deepen our bond with patience and care."

Belief in Us: "I believe in us and the potential of our relationship, trusting in our ability to navigate challenges and celebrate our successes together."

"The ones that stand by and watch you thrive are always the ones you can never decline." ~ Taelations

"The ones you stand by wouldn't hurt or manipulate you, they'll work with you and help you gain not overweight toxic ones gotta go, healthy ones matter the most." ~ Taelations

"Never apologize for others' wrongs. The most you can do is apologize for what you did right for them to do you wrong." ~ Taelations

Book 2 to be continued...

www.ingramcontent.com/pod-product-compliance
Lightning Source LLC
Chambersburg PA
CBHW071232160426
43196CB00012B/2490